Collins English Library

Series editors: K R Cripwe

A library of graded readers for stud
reluctant native readers. The book
Structure, vocabulary, idiom and s
principles laid down in detail in A
books are listed below according to
words and appropriate structures,
5: 2000 words and 6: 2500 words. '
accompanied by a cassette.

Level Four

The White South *Hammond Innes*
A Christmas Carol *Charles Dickens*
King Solomon's Mines*
H Rider Haggard
Jane Eyre *Charlotte Brontë*
Pride and Prejudice *Jane Austen*
Dr Jekyll and Mr Hyde*
R L Stevenson
Huckleberry Finn *Mark Twain*
Landslide *Desmond Bagley*
Nothing is the Number When You
Die *Joan Fleming*
The African Child *Camara Laye*
The Lovely Lady and other Stories
D H Lawrence
Airport International *Brian Moynahan*
The Secret Sharer and other Sea
Stories *Joseph Conrad*
Death in Vienna? *K E Rowlands*
Hostage Tower* *Alistair MacLean*
The Potter's Wheel *Chukwuemeka Ike*
Tina Turner *Stephen Rabley*
Campbell's Kingdom *Hammond Innes*
Barchester Towers *Anthony Trollope*
Rear Window *Cornell Woolrich*

Level Five

The Guns of Navarone
Alistair MacLean

Geordie *David Walker*
Wuthering Heights *Emily Brontë*
Where Eagles Dare *Alistair MacLean*
Wreck of the Mary Deare
Hammond Innes
I Know My Love *Catherine Gaskin*
The Mayor of Casterbridge
Thomas Hardy
Sense and Sensibility *Jane Austen*
The Eagle has Landed *Jack Higgins*
Middlemarch *George Eliot*
Victory *Joseph Conrad*
Experiences of Terror* *Roland John*
Japan: Islands in the Mist
Peter Milward
The Freedom Trap *Desmond Bagley*

Level Six

Doctor Zhivago *Boris Pasternak*
The Glory Boys *Gerald Seymour*
In the Shadow of Man *Jane Goodall*
Harry's Game *Gerald Seymour*
House of a Thousand Lanterns
Victoria Holt
Hard Times *Charles Dickens*
Sons and Lovers *D H Lawrence*
The Dark Frontier *Eric Ambler*
Vanity Fair *William Thackeray*
Inspector Ghote Breaks an Egg
H R F Keating

Collins English Library Level 3

OSCAR WILDE

Short Stories

Contents

Abridged and simplified by Jen Macdonell

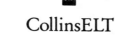

CollinsELT

A Division of HarperCollins*Publishers*

This edition © Jan Macdonell 1988

Collins ELT
HarperCollins Publishers
77-85 Fulham Palace Road
London W6 8JB

Printed by Martin's of Berwick

First published in Collins English Library, 1988
Reprinted: 1989 (twice), 1990, 1992

ISBN 0 00 370178 6

Cover illustration by Mario Minichiello
Cover design by Danny Lim
Illustrations by Morna Whyte

The Nightingale and the Rose

"She said she would dance with me if I brought her red roses," cried the young Student, "but in all my garden there is no red rose."

On a branch in the old orange tree, a Nightingale sang her songs of love, but the Student did not hear the bird. When the Nightingale heard his voice, she stopped singing and wondered.

"No red roses in all my garden!" the Student cried, and his beautiful eyes filled with sadness. "Oh! happiness comes from such little things! No red roses!"

"Here, at last, is a true lover," said the Nightingale. "Night after night I have sung about him, but I didn't know him. Night after night I have told his story to the stars, and now I see him. His hair is as dark as the night, and his lips are rose-red, but his face is white, and sadness has set her mark upon it."

"The Prince is giving a big party tomorrow night," said the young Student quietly, "and

5

my love will be there. If I bring a red rose she will dance with me till daybreak. She will rest her head against me, and I will hold her hand in mine. But there is no red rose in my garden, so I shall sit lonely, and she will pass me by. She will not notice me and my heart will break."

"Oh yes, here is the true lover," said the Nightingale. "I only sing of sadness, but he feels its hurt. To me, love is happiness: to him it is emptiness. It is a greater treasure than jewels, but it cannot be bought with gold."

"The music will play," said the young Student. "My love will dance lightly and her feet will not touch the floor. But with me she will not dance, because I have no red rose for her," and he threw himself down on the grass, put his head in hands, and cried.

"Why is he crying?" asked the animals and the flowers in the garden.

"He is crying because of a red rose," said the Nightingale.

"For a red rose!" they cried; and they laughed out loud.

But the Nightingale understood the secret of the Student's sadness, and she sat silent in the orange tree, and thought about the mystery of love.

Suddenly she flew into the air, and sailed across the garden like a shadow.

In the centre of the garden was a beautiful

Rose-tree, and when the Nightingale saw it, she flew over to it and landed on a branch.

"Give me a red rose," she cried, "and I will sing you my sweetest song."

But the Tree shook its head.

"My roses are white," it answered, "whiter than the snow upon the Mountain. But go to my brother and perhaps he will give you what you want."

So the Nightingale flew over to the other Rose-tree.

"Give me a red rose," she cried, "and I will sing you my sweetest song."

But the Tree shook its head.

"My roses are yellow," it answered, "yellower than the flowers in the summer fields. But go to my brother who grows below the Student's window, and perhaps he will give you what you want."

So the Nightingale flew over to the Rose-tree that was growing below the Student's window.

"Give me a red rose," she cried, "and I will sing you my sweetest song."

But the Tree shook its head.

"My roses are red," it answered, "as red as the sunset. But I am still cold from the Winter winds and the storms have broken my branches, and I shall have no roses at all this year ..."

"One red rose is all I want," cried the

8

Nightingale, "only one red rose. How can I get one?"

"There is a way," answered the Tree, "but it is so fearful that I dare not tell it to you."

"Tell it to me," said the Nightingale. "I am not afraid."

"If you want a red rose," said the Tree, "you must build it out of music by moonlight, and redden it with your own heart's blood. Look at these thorns along my branches – they are as deadly as the points of knives. You must sing to me with your body against a thorn. All night you must sing to me, and the thorn must enter your heart, and your life-blood must pass into my body and become mine."

"Death is a great price to pay for a red rose," cried the Nightingale, "and Life is very dear to all. It is wonderful to sit in the green wood and watch the Sun and The Moon and smell the flowers. But Love is better than Life, and the heart of a man is surely more valuable than the heart of a bird."

So once again she rose into the air and like a shadow she sailed through the trees.

The young Student was still lying on the grass, and his eyes were still wet.

"Be happy," cried the Nightingale, "be happy: you shall have your red rose. I will btuild it out of music by moonlight, and redden it with my own heart's blood. In

9

return, I ask you to be a true lover, because Love is the greatest power in the world."

The Student looked up from the grass and listened. But he could not understand what the Nightingale was saying to him. He only knew the things that were written down in books.

But the old orange tree in the garden understood, and felt sad, because he liked the Nightingale who lived in his branches.

"Sing me one last song," he said very quietly. "I shall feel lonely when you are gone."

So the Nightingale sang to the orange-tree and her voice was like clear water from a silver cup.

When she finished her song, the Student got up and pulled a note-book and a pencil out of his pocket.

"The song has form," he said to himself, as he walked through the garden, "but does it have feeling? I don't think so. In fact, the Nightingale is like most artists – she thinks only of music and herself. But she has some beautiful notes in her voice. It's sad that they don't mean anything, or do any real good for anyone." And he went into his room and lay down on his bed, and began to think of his love; and after a time he fell asleep.

And when the Moon shone in the night sky,

the Nightingale flew to the Rose-tree and pressed her body against the thorn. All night long she sang with her body against the thorn, and the cold silver Moon listened. All night long she sang and the thorn went deeper and deeper into her body, and her life-blood went slowly from her.

She sang first of the birth of Love in the heart of a boy and a girl. On the top branch of the Rose-tree there slowly flowered a wonderful rose, as song followed song. It was very, very white at first.

But the Tree cried to the Nightingale, "Press closer, little Nightingale or the Day will come before the rose is finished."

So the Nightingale pressed closer against the thorn, and her song grew louder and louder, as she sang of the love between a man and a woman.

And a pink colour came into the leaves of the rose, like the pink in the face of a girl when her husband kissed her for the first time. But the thorn was not yet at her heart, so the rose's heart remained white. Only a Nightingale's heart's-blood could redden the heart of a rose.

And the Tree cried to the Nightingale, "Press closer, little Nightingale, or the Day will come before the rose is finished."

So the Nightingale pressed closer against

the thorn, and the thorn touched her heart. And her song grew wilder because she sang of the Love that does not die.

And the wonderful rose became dark red, like the rose of the eastern sky at sunrise.

But the Nightingale's voice was failing and a curtain of darkness began to fall over her eyes. Her song became weaker and weaker. She could almost sing no more.

Then she gave one last note of music. The white Moon heard it and stayed in the sky. The red rose heard it and opened in the cold morning air. The hills and the rivers and the sea heard it.

"Look, Look!" cried the Tree, "The rose is finished now," but the Nightingale made no answer. She was lying dead in the long grass, with the thorn in her heart.

And at mid-day the Student opened his window and looked out.

"What a wonderful piece of luck!" he cried. "Here is a red rose! I have never seen any rose like it in all my life. It so beautiful that it must have a long name," and he picked it from the Tree. Then he put on his hat and ran up to his love's house with the rose in his hand.

She was sitting in the doorway, and her little dog was at her feet.

"You said you would dance with me if I brought you a red rose," cried the Student.

"Here is the reddest rose in the world. You will wear it tonight next to your heart. As we dance together I will tell you how much I love you."

But the girl's face darkened.

"I'm sorry but it's the wrong colour for my dress," she answered, "and in any case, a certain young man has sent me some real jewels. And everyone knows that the jewels cost far more than flowers."

"Well, you're not very kind. You should thank me," said the Student angrily; and he threw the rose into the street and a car went over it.

"Not very kind!" said the girl. "I can tell you something. You are rough and thoughtless. And after all, who are you? Only a Student. You have no silver on your shoes like rich young men have." And she got up from her chair and went into the house.

"Love doesn't make any sense," said the Student as he walked away. "It's useless – it can't prove anything. And it's always telling us things that are not true. In fact, it's a waste of time. It's much better to study something useful."

So he returned to his room and pulled down a great dusty book about science, and began to read it.

The Happy Prince

High above the city stood the Happy Prince. He was made of gold. His eyes were two bright blue stones. He had a sword with a dark red stone at the top

People often looked up at him. "He is very beautiful," said the people of the town as they passed below.

"Stop crying," said a mother to her son. "Why can't you be like the Happy Prince? He never cries."

"I am glad there's someone in the world who is happy," said a sad old man looking up at the Happy Prince.

One day a black and white bird flew over the city. His friends were in Africa for the winter. He stayed in England because he was in love. He wanted to stay with his new friend. But after some time he grew tired of his friend. he decided to fly to Africa.

He flew all day long, and at night time he arrived at the city.

"Where will I spend the night?" he asked himself.

Then he saw the Prince in his high place above the city.

"I'll sleep up there. It's a fine place with plenty of fresh air," he said. And he landed just between the feet of the Happy Prince.

"I have a golden bedroom," he said softly to himself as he looked round, and prepared to go to sleep. But as he was going to sleep, a large drop of water fell on his head.

"What a strange thing!" he cried. "There isn't a cloud in the sky, the stars are clear and bright, and it's raining. The weather in England is terrible!"

Then another drop fell.

"This place is no good, if it can't keep the rain off," he said. "I must look for another place to spend the night."

He nearly flew away, but then a third drop fell. He looked up and saw – Ah! What did he see?

The eyes of the Happy Prince were full of water. His face was wet. He looked so beautiful in the moonlight. The bird was very sad for him.

"Who are you?" he asked.

"I am the Happy Prince."

"Then why are you crying?" asked the bird. "I am all wet now."

"When I was alive I had a human heart. I was always very happy. People called me the Happy Prince. Then I died. The people put me up here. From this high place I can see all the bad things and the sad things in the city. Now I want to cry when I see these things."

"Far away," continued the Prince in his low, musical voice, "far away in a little street there is a poor house. One of the windows is open. I can see a woman sitting at a table. Her face is thin. She is making a dress for the King's daughter. In a bed in the corner of the room, her little boy is lying ill. His body is very hot. He is asking for oranges. His mother has nothing to give him – only water – so he is crying. Little bird, will you take the red stone from my sword and give it to her?"

"But my friends are waiting for me in Africa."

"Little bird, I can't move from here," said the Prince. "Won't you stay with me for one night? The boy is so thirsty, and his mother is so sad."

"I don't think I like little boys" said the bird. "Last summer near the river, two boys threw stones at me. They didn't hit me. But they weren't friendly."

But the Happy Prince looked so sad. The bird was sorry. "It's very cold here, but I'll stay for one night," he said at last.

"Thank you, little bird," said the Prince.

So the bird picked out the red stone from the Prince's sword and flew away over the roofs of the city.

He passed by the King's house. A beautiful girl looked out of an open window. "I hope my dress will be ready for the party. The dressmaker is very slow. She must finish it quickly so it is ready."

At last the bird came to the poor house and looked in. The boy was in bed, very hot. His mother was asleep in her chair. She was very tired. He went through the window, and put the red stone on the table beside the woman. Then he flew gently round the bed. "Now I feel cool," said the boy, "I'm getting better"; and he fell asleep again, more comfortable.

Then the bird flew back to the Happy Prince. "It's strange," he said, "It's a cold night, but I feel nice and warm now."

"That's because you have done something good," said the Prince.

The next morning, the bird flew down to the Happy Prince. "I'm just going to Africa now," he said.

"Little bird, won't you stay with me for one more night?"

"But my friends are waiting for me in Africa," answered the little bird.

"Little bird," said the Prince, "far across the

city I see a young man in a cold room at the top of a house. He's working at a table full of papers. He's trying to finish a play, but it's too cold to write any more. he has no fire in his house and he's ill with hunger."

"I'll stay with you one more night," said the bird, who really had a good heart. "Shall I take him another red stone?"

"I have no red stones now," said the Prince; "My eyes are all I have left. They are made of unusual blue stones. They came from India a thousand years ago. Take one of them and take it to him. He'll sell it and buy food and firewood, and then finish his play."

"Dear Prince," said the bird, "I can't do that," and he began to cry.

"Little bird," said the Prince, "do as I say."

So the bird took out the Prince's eye, and flew to the student's cold room. He went in through a hole in the roof. The young man's head was down in his hands. When he looked up, he saw the beautiful, blue stone on the table.

"This is from someone who likes my work," he said. "Now I can finish my play," and he looked quite happy.

The next day the little black and white bird flew down to the sea. He sat on a big ship and called, "I am going to Africa."

When the moon rose, he flew back to the Happy Prince.

19

"I've come to say goodbye," he said.

"Little bird," said the Prince, "won't you stay with me one more night?"

"It's winter," answered the bird. "And the snow will soon be here. It is warm in Africa and my friends are waiting for me there. I must leave you, dear Prince. I'll come back next spring, and I'll bring you two beautiful jewels in place of those you have given away."

"In the square below," said the Happy Prince, "there is a little girl. She's trying to sell matches, but the matches are wet. Her father will beat her if she does not bring home some money. She has no shoes, and nothing on her head. She's very cold and very sad. Take out my other eye, and give it to her, and her father will not beat her."

"I'll stay with you one more night," said the bird, "but I can't take out your eye because then you won't be able to see."

"Little bird," said the Prince, "do as I say."

So he took out the Prince's other eye, and quickly went to the little girl. He put the jewel into the girl's hand. "What a lovely bit of glass," she cried, and ran home, laughing.

Then the black and white bird came back to the Prince. "Now you can't see anything," he said, "so I'll stay with you always."

"No, little bird," said the poor Prince, "you must go to Africa."

20

"I'll stay with you always," said the bird, and he slept at the Prince's feet.

All the next day, the bird stayed near the Prince, and told him stories of strange lands. He told him of the birds and the animals and the rivers in those places. And of the people and the food in far away countries.

"Dear little bird," said the Prince, "you tell me of wonderful things. But one thing is more wonderful than anything. And that is the sadness of the people. Fly over the city, little bird, and tell me what you see there."

So the bird flew over the great city. He saw rich people in their beautiful homes, with poor people sitting outside. He saw the white faces of very hungry children. He saw two boys under a bridge, trying to keep warm. "How hungry we are!" they said.

Then the bird flew back and told the Prince what he saw.

"I'm covered with fine gold," said the Prince. "You must take it off, leaf by leaf, and give it to the poor. People always think that gold will make them happy."

The bird picked off the gold, leaf after leaf. The Prince then looked grey and wasn't bright any more. The bird took leaf after leaf of gold to the poor. The children's faces grew brighter, and they laughed and played games in the street. "We'll have bread now!" they cried.

Then the snow came, and then the ice. The streets were bright and shiny, like silver.

The poor little bird grew colder and colder. He could not leave the Prince; he loved him too well.

But at last he knew he was going to die. He flew up to the Prince, with difficulty.

"Goodbye, dear Prince," he said very quietly.

"I'm glad that you are going to Africa at last, little bird," said the Prince. "You've stayed too long here."

"I'm not going to Africa," said the bird, "I'm going to die."

He kissed the Happy Prince, and fell down dead at his feet.

At that moment there was a strange noise inside the Prince. His heart broke in two.

Early the next morning, the town leaders were walking in the square below. They looked up and said "The Happy Prince looks very bad today."

"Yes, the stone has fallen from his sword, his eyes have gone, and he is no longer golden. In fact, he looks like a poor man."

"And there is a dead bird at his feet. We must make a law. Birds are not allowed to die here."

So they pulled down the Happy Prince.

"Because he is no longer beautiful he is no

longer useful," said one of the town leaders. "Let's put the Happy Prince in a big fire and use the metal to make a new statue."

The leaders of the town argued and argued.

"It must be a statue of me," said one.

"No, no. It must be of me," said another.

And they argued and argued. Each one wanted to be famous. Each one wanted a statue of himself.

"What a strange thing!" said the man who made the big fire. "This broken heart will not burn. We must throw it away." So they threw it onto the rubbish, where the dead bird was also lying.

Some time later, the King spoke to the people of the town.

"Bring me the two most valuable things in the city," said the King. And the people brought him the broken heart and the dead bird – the two things that understood people's sadness.

The Selfish Giant

Every afternoon, as they were coming from school, the children went to play in the garden of the Giant's castle.

It was a large, lovely garden, with soft green grass. Here and there over the grass stood beautiful flowers like stars. There were twelve apple trees – in the Springtime they broke out into pretty flowers of pink and white. In the Autumn they carried rich fruit. The birds sat on the trees and sang sweetly.

One day, after seven years, the Giant came back to his castle. When he arrived, he saw the children playing in the garden. The tops of their heads only came halfway up his legs. The Giant was very big. To the children, he seemed as tall as the sky.

"What are you doing here?" he cried in an angry voice.

"My own garden is my own garden," said the Giant, "and I will let nobody play in it but myself." The children ran away.

KEEP OUT
OF THIS
GARDEN!

He built a high wall around the garden and put up a big notice:

**KEEP OUT OF
THIS GARDEN!**

The Giant thought only of himself. Self, self, self.

The children now had nowhere to play.

"The Giant is very selfish," they said. They tried to play on the road, but the road was dusty and full of hard stones. They didn't like playing there.

After school, they walked round the high wall, but now they couldn't see the beautiful garden inside.

Then the Spring came, and all over the country there were flowers and little birds. Only in the garden of the Selfish Giant it was still winter. The birds didn't sing in it and the trees grew no leaves, because there were no children. Once, a beautiful flower put its head out from the grass, but when it saw the notice, it made its way back into the ground again and went to sleep.

The only people who were happy were the Snow and the Ice.

"Spring has forgotten this garden," they said, "so we will live here all the year round."

The Snow covered up the grass with her great white coat, and the Ice painted all the trees silver. Then they asked the North Wind to stay with them, and he came. He crashed around all day in the cold garden.

"This is a very nice place," he said. "We must ask the Rain to visit."

So the Rain came. Every day for three hours he banged on the castle roof till it almost broke. Then he ran round the garden as fast as he could. He was dressed in grey, and his breath was like ice.

"I cannot understand why Spring is late in coming," said the Selfish Giant, as he looked out at his cold, white garden.

But Spring never came, nor the Summer. The Autumn gave golden fruit to every garden, but to the Giant's garden she gave none. So it was always Winter there, and the North Wind and the Rain and the Ice and Snow danced about through the trees.

One morning, the Giant was lying awake in bed when he heard some lovely music. It was really only a little yellow singing-bird outside his window. But to him it seemed the most beautiful music in the world.

Then the Rain stopped dancing over his head and the North Wind stopped blowing. A lovely smell came in through his bedroom window.

"I believe the Spring has come at last," said the Giant; and he jumped out of bed and looked out.

What did he see?

He saw a most wonderful sight. The children were sitting in the branches of the trees. In every tree there was a little child. The trees were covered in flowers again, and they moved their arms gently from side to side above the children's heads. The birds were flying about and singing with happiness. The flowers were looking through the green grass and laughing.

But in one corner of the garden it was still winter. In that part of the garden a little boy was standing. He was small, so he could not reach up to the branches of the tree. He was walking around the tree, crying. The poor tree was still covered with snow and ice, and the North Wind was blowing around it.

"Climb up, little boy," said the tree, and bent its branches down as low as it could; but the boy was too small.

And the Giant's hard heart softened as he looked out.

"I have been thinking only of myself! Now I know why Spring would not come here. It's because I've been selfish."

He went quietly downstairs and opened the front door of his castle very softly. He went into the garden. But the children looked up at him and ran away. The garden became winter again.

Only the little boy didn't run. He was crying and he didn't see the Giant coming. The Giant came up behind him quietly and picked him up gently in his great hand. He put him into the tree.

At once, the tree broke out into flowers and the birds came and sang on it. The boy held out his two arms and threw them around the Giant's neck and kissed him.

For a moment, the other children watched in silence. Then they ran back into the garden. And Spring came with them.

"It is your garden now, little children," said the Giant, and he broke down the wall round the garden.

All day long the children played in the garden and in the evening they said goodbye to the Giant.

"But where is your little friend?" he asked: "the boy that I put into the tree?"

He loved the boy best because he kissed the Giant.

"We don't know," answered the children, "he's gone away."

"You must tell him to be sure to come here

29

tomorrow," said the Giant.

But the children said they didn't know where he lived. The Giant felt very sad.

Every afternoon after school the children came and played with the Giant. But the little boy that the Giant loved was never seen again.

Years passed and the Giant grew very old and weak. He could not play any more, so he sat in his big armchair. He looked at his garden, and watched the children playing.

"I have many beautiful flowers," he said, "but you children are the most beautiful flowers of all."

One winter morning he looked out of his window. He didn't hate the Winter now. He knew it was only Spring asleep – the flowers were only resting.

Suddenly he saw a strange thing. In a corner of the garden there was a tree. It was covered with lovely white flowers. Its branches were golden and silver fruit was hanging from them.

The little boy the Giant loved was standing under the tree. The Giant ran downstairs and out into the garden. He ran across the grass and when he was near the boy he said, "Who has hurt you?"

In each of the boy's hands there was a hole. And in each foot there was a hole.

The Giant looked down at the little boy, and

cried,

"Who has dared hurt you? Tell me so I can kill him with my sword."

"No!" answered the little boy, "these are marks of Love."

"Who are you?" cried the Giant, bending down before the little child.

And the child smiled up at the Giant. He said to the Giant, "You let me play in your garden. Today you will come with me and play in my garden, up in the sky."

The children ran into the garden that afternoon. They found the Giant lying dead under the tree, all covered with white flowers.

Lord Arthur Savile's Crime

1

Once upon a time Lady Windermere had a big party for all her friends. That evening, her house was full of people. They were enjoying the music and the food. There were princesses and scientists and artists.

Suddenly Lady Windermere looked around the room and said to Lady Paisley,

"Where is my fortune-teller?"

"Really! You have a fortune-teller?" said Lady Paisley.

"Yes, he comes to read my hand twice a week, and he says very interesting things about it."

"How unusual!" said Lady Paisley. "He tells your future I suppose?"

"Yes, the good things and the bad things — about your past and your future. You must meet him. Ah, there he is. Now, Mr Podgers, I want you to read Lady Paisley's hand. Lady Paisley, let Mr Podgers see your hand."

Mr Podgers had a fat face and a weak smile. But behind his gold glasses he had deep, dark eyes that seemed to see into you.

Mr Podgers took the Duchess's right hand and looked carefully at it.

"You will live to a great age and be very happy," said Mr Podgers. "You like comfort and you like being rich. You will never be poor."

"Excellent," said Lady Windermere. "Now you must read Lady Flora's hand."

Mr Podgers studied Lady Flora's hand.

"Ah, you play music. You love to play music. And you also have a great love of animals."

"Quite true," said Lady Windermere. "Lady Flora has twenty four dogs at home. And she plays music everyday."

Then Mr Podgers read some more hands. Everybody showed great surprise as he told them about their past and future.

One man became very angry when Mr Podgers read his hand.

"You have great money difficulties," said Mr Podgers.

"You want to marry a rich lady for her money. She is old and sick. But she will live longer than you."

The man left the party angrily.

"It's true," Some of the people said, "It's true. He lost all his money in business. And now he wants to marry a country lady."

Another man spoke. "I'm his doctor," he said, "and I know he has a bad heart. He has only a year to live."

Some people were afraid to let Mr Podgers read their hands. They didn't want other people to know about their past or their future.

Lord Arthur Savile was watching Mr Podgers with great interest. He wanted to know about his own future but was worried about asking Mr Podgers. Lady Windermere said, "Lord Arthur, Mr Podgers must read your hand. He may tell us some interesting things. Then I can tell your future wife, tomorrow when she comes to lunch."

"I'm sure I keep no secret from Sybil."

"Let's find out!" said Lady Windermere. "Mr Podgers, please look at Lord Arthur's hand. Be sure and tell us something nice."

But when Mr Podgers saw Lord Arthur's hand his face grew strangely white and he said nothing. He seemed worried. Lord Arthur noticed Mr Podger's unusual silence.

Suddenly Mr Podgers dropped Lord Arthur's right hand and quickly took up his left hand and studied it very closely.

For a moment, Mr Podger's face became white. He began to shake with fear. Then, at last, he said with a forced smile, "The hand of a very nice young man."

"Of course, it is," answered Lady Windermere, "but will he be a nice husband? That is what I want to know."

"All nice young men are," said Mr Podgers.

"But I want to know more. What is going to happen to Lord Arthur."

"Well, Lord Arthur will go on a long journey."

"Oh, yes, after his marriage, of course."

"And lose one of his family," said Mr Podgers.

"Not his sister, I hope?" said Lady Windermere.

"Certainly not his sister," answered Mr Podgers. "Someone else – in his family."

"Well, I am very unhappy," said Lady Windermere. "I have nothing to tell Sybil tomorrow – nothing of any interest at all."

The Lady Windermere left the room with the others, to have dinner.

All this time, Lord Arthur was standing near the fire, feeling unhappy and worried. He thought about Sybil Merton, and hated the idea that anything could come between them.

Was the future written in his hand? Did the lines on his hand tell of a crime, or that he was a criminal? Surely it was not possible! Did Mr Podgers read a dark secret in his hands?

Suddenly Mr Podgers entered the room.

When he saw Lord Arthur standing there, unhappy and worried, he was very surprised – his face became a yellow colour.

"Mr Podgers," said Lord Arthur. "I have a question I want to ask."

"Question? There is no time for questions," said Mr Podgers quickly.

"Yes, there is. You must answer this question: what did you see in the lines of my hand? I must know," said Lord Arthur.

"I told you everything I saw in your hand," said Mr Podgers. His voice was full of fear.

"I don't believe you. I will give you a lot of money if you tell me. You must tell me."

"All right," said Mr Podgers at last. "Is the door closed?"

2

Ten minutes later, Lord Arthur ran out of the house. His face was white, his eyes wild with sadness. He walked for a long time through the dark streets of London.

Murder! This is what the fortune-teller saw in Lord Arthur's future. Murder! Mr Podgers told Lord Arthur that he would kill someone. That he *must* kill someone! That he would never be happy until he did it. But when? Who? How? Everything around him seemed to know it. He was full of fear and worry. What could he do? He walked and walked in the darkness, not really knowing where he was going. As the birds were beginning to sing, he arrived home.

3

When Lord Arthur woke, it was twelve o'clock, and the mid-day sun was shining brightly through his window. It was a very beautiful day. He drank some hot chocolate and then had a bath. After breakfast, he had a cigarette and looked at a photograph of Sybil Merton. She was very beautiful.

Lord Arthur felt very sad. How could he marry her, when his head was full of murder? How could they be happy together? He must change the day of the marriage. It must happen later, after the murder was done.

The thought of murder made Lord Arthur ill. But Mr Podger said it was his only chance of happiness. That was the dark secret in his hands. His happiness, his future with Sybil, everything – he had to murder someone or all this was lost.

So he thought about a person to murder. It was difficult, because he had no enemies. At last he made a list of his friends and family. In the end he chose his aunt, Lady Clementina Beauchamp. He decided to kill her.

He decided to poison her. He would give her something to eat or drink which would kill her. It was a safe, sure and quiet way to kill her.

Then he went to the chemist to buy the poison. At first, the chemist did not want to give him the poison. Lord Arthur said it was for a big, bad, dangerous dog. The chemist soon gave him the poison.

Lord Arthur put the medicine into a pretty, silver box and drove at once to Lady Clementina's house.

"Well," cried the old lady when he entered the room, "why haven't you been to see me all this time?"

"I've been very busy," said Lord Arthur, smiling.

"I have few visitors these days, you know. Who wants to come and see me, a sick, old woman? Doctors come, but they're no use at all. They can't fix anything."

"I've brought something just right for your illness. It's a wonderful thing, made by an American. You must promise to try it." And Lord Arthur brought the little box out of his pocket, and handed it to her.

"Well, it's a very nice box, Arthur. Is it really for me? It's like a sweet. I'll eat it at once."

"No, no, Lady Clem," cried Lord Arthur, "you mustn't take it until you are ill. Wait till you feel ill and then take it. The result will surprise you."

"I would like to take it now," said Lady Clementina. "I'm sure it is very nice. I hate doctors, but I love medicines. But I'll keep it until my next attack."

"And when will that be?" asked Lord Arthur. "Will it be soon?"

"I hope not for a week. But one never knows."

"You are sure to have an attack by the end of the month then, Lady Clem?"

"Probably, yes. You are very kind today, Arthur, thinking of me in this way. But now you must run away because I am having lunch with some uninteresting people. I don't want to be late. Give my love to Sybil and thank you for the American medicine."

"You won't forget to take it, Lady Clem, will you?" said Lord Arthur, leaving.

"Of course, I won't. And I shall write and tell you if I want any more."

Lord Arthur left the house feeling very happy.

That night Lord Arthur met Sybil Merton. He told her the marriage must be later. He told her not to worry about the future.

40

Everything would come right, but she must wait a little.

Sybil felt very happy that evening when she saw Lord Arthur, but when she heard the news she was very sad. She could not understand the need to change the date of the marriage. But Lord Arthur could not change his plans to kill Lady Clementina.

The next day he left for Italy.

4

In Venice he met his brother. They spent two weeks together in the beautiful city. But Lord Arthur was not happy.

Every day he looked at the newspaper hoping to find news of Lady Clementina's death. Every day there was nothing.

Then, at last, the news came – Lady Clementina was dead. One night after dinner she felt ill. The next morning she was dead.

Lord Arthur returned to London completely happy. Everything was all right now. The murder which Mr Podgers saw in Lord Arthur's hand – in his future – was now over. Now he could be happy.

Lady Clementina left her house to him and all the furniture in it. But, most important of all, he loved Sybil very, very much. Now he could marry her, and they made new plans for the marriage.

One day soon after his return, Lord Arthur and Sybil were cleaning up at Lady Clementina's house.

"Look what I have found," said Sybil, smiling. "A beautiful little silver box. Can I have it?"

Lord Arthur looked surprised. The murder was nearly out of his thoughts.

"Of course you can have it, Sybil. I gave it to poor Lady Clem myself."

"And can I have the sweet, too?"

"Sweet?" said Lord Arthur, his face turning very white. "What do you mean?"

"There's a sweet in the box, that's all. It's old and dirty. I won't eat it. What's wrong, Arthur? You look ill!"

Lord Arthur quickly took the box. He looked at the 'sweet' inside. So, Lady Clementina died a natural death after all!

He threw the sweet into the fire, and sat down in the chair with an unhappy cry. Now he had to begin again – to find somebody to murder.

5

Sybil's father was very unhappy to hear the

marriage plans were changed again. Her mother wanted her to forget about marrying Lord Arthur – he was becoming too difficult. Perhaps it was better to stop the marriage plans, and not marry Sybil at all. Then Sybil would be very unhappy. Oh! what could he do?

That evening he had dinner with his brother. Then he walked along the River Thames until midnight. It was very dark. He sat by the river for a long time. At two o'clock he got up and walked a little more.

He saw a man standing by the wall very near the river. Suddenly he realised it was Mr Podgers – with his fat face and gold glasses and his weak smile.

Lord Arthur stopped. He had an idea. He went up behind Mr Podgers and quickly took him by the legs. He threw him into the river. There was a heavy splash, then all was still and quiet.

Lord Arthur looked over the wall. He could see nothing.

"Have you dropped anything, sir? said someone behind him suddenly.

"Nothing important," he answered, a smile on his lips.

For the next two or three days Lord Arthur felt both hopeful and worried. There were moments when he thought Mr Podgers might walk into the room. He went twice to Mr. Podgers house but could not ring the bell. He wanted to be sure that Mr Podgers was not there, but was afraid to find out.

And then the news came. He read in the newspaper:

> *"Yesterday morning at seven o'clock , the body of Mr Septimus R. Podgers, the famous fortune-teller was found on the banks of the river Thames. It is believed that he took his own life. He was 65 years old."*

Lord Arthur ran as fast as possible to Sybil's house.

"My dear Sybil," cried Lord Arthur. "Let's get married tomorrow!"

"What?! The cake is not even ordered!" said Sybil, laughing and crying at the same time.

6

Lord Arthur and Sybil were married three weeks later. The church was crowded. Everyone was happy. It was a wonderful day.

Some years afterwards, Lady Windermere came to visit Lord Arthur and Sybil.

"Are you happy, Sybil?" Lady Windermere

asked her hostess.

"Of course I am happy. Aren't you?"

"I have no time to be happy, Sybil."

"Oh, dear," said Sybil.

"Do you remember that man Mr Podgers? He wasn't a *real* fortune- teller, you know."

"You mustn't say anything against fortune-telling, Lady Windermere. Arthur believes in it very strongly."

"Really," said Lady Windermere, surprised.

"Ask him. Here he is," said Sybil, as Lord Arthur came up the garden with some roses in his hand.

"Lord Arthur, you don't really believe in fortune-telling, do you?"

"Of course, I do" said the young man, smiling.

"But why?"

"Because it has made my life very happy," he said quite quietly.

"How has it made your life happy?" asked Lady Windermere.

"By giving me Sybil," he answered, handing his wife the roses and looking into her beautiful eyes.

"What rubbish!" cried Lady Windermere. "I never heard such rubbish in all my life."

The Poor Millionaire

"No!" The old army man sat up straight in his armchair, and banged the floor with his stick.

"Come and ask me again when you've got ten thousand pounds, Hughie. Then you can think about marrying my daughter Laura. Not before."

Hughie was not very brainy. He never said a clever or even an unfriendly thing in his life. But he was wonderfully good-looking, with his thick brown hair, his open face, and his grey eyes.

He could do almost anything – except make money. He tried the money markets, but he was a chicken among lions. He tried selling tea, whisky – everything. But in the end, he became nothing: a nice young man with a nice face – but no job.

To make things worse, he was in love with Laura Merton, and she loved him.

One morning, on his way to Laura's house, he stopped to visit a great friend of his, Alan Trevor. Trevor was a painter. He was a

strange, rough man with a red face and a red beard. He painted very well and people always wanted his pictures.

He liked Hughie very much. He liked his good looks and his bright nature. So Hughie often visited him at work.

When Hughie came in, he found Trevor working. Trevor was just finishing a big picture of a very poor man. The old man was standing in a corner of the room. He looked very tired and old and quite ill. He was wearing an old brown coat with holes in it; one hand was holding a stick, the other was asking for money.

"What a wonderful man!" said Hughie quietly, as he shook hands with his friend.

"A wonderful man?" said Trevor. "Of course! You don't meet people like this man every day."

"Poor old fellow," said Hughie, "he looks sad! But I suppose his face makes him money"

"Certainly," answered Trevor. "You don't want a poor old man to look happy, do you?"

"How much does he get for sitting?" asked Hughie.

"A pound an hour."

"And how much do you get for your picture?"

"Oh, for this I get two thousand."

"Pounds?"

"Of course."

"Well, I think this man should get part of that money," cried Hughie, laughing. "He's working as hard as you are."

"Rubbish!" said Alan. "I have to buy the paint and stand up all day. It's very hard work. Now, stop talking – I'm busy. Have a cigarette and keep quiet."

After some time, Trevor went out to meet a visitor. When he left the room, the old man had a little rest. He looked sad and hungry.

Hughie felt in his pockets to find some money. He had a pound coin and a ten-pound note.

"Poor old man," he thought to himself, "he wants it more than I do. But it means no nice things for me for a week." And he walked across the room and put the ten-pound note into the poor man's hand.

The old man smiled and said thank you.

That night Hughie went to the club. He met Trevor.

"Well, Alan, did you finish the picture all right?" he asked as he lit his cigarette.

"Completely finished," answered Trevor. "You know, the old man I was painting was very interested in you. I had to tell him about you – who you are, where you live, how much money you have, –"

"My dear Alan," cried Hughie. "He'll be at my front door when I get home. I wish I could do something for him. He looked unhappy. I have a lot of clothes at home – do you think he'd like them? His clothes are very old."

"He looks very good in those clothes," said Trevor. "But I'll tell him of your offer. And now tell me how Laura is. The old man was quite interested in her."

"You don't mean you talked to him about her?" cried Hughie.

"Certainly I did. He knows all about Laura, and her father, and the £10,000."

"You told that old man about my troubles?" cried Hughie.

"Don't look so angry, dear boy," said Trevor, smiling. "That poor old man, as you call him, is one of the richest men in Europe. He could buy all London tomorrow. He has a house in every capital city. He eats off gold plates."

"What do you mean?" cried Hughie in an excited voice.

"I mean what I say," said Trevor. "The old man you saw today is Baron Hausberg. He's a great friend of mine. He buys all my pictures. He wanted me to paint him as a poor old man. So he dressed in my old clothes and I painted him."

"Baron Hausberg!" cried Hughie. "Oh

dear! I gave him ten pounds!"

"You gave him ten pounds!?" shouted Trevor, and broke into loud laughter.

"He must think I'm very strange," said Hughie.

"Not at all. He was very happy when you left. And he was very interested in you. He'll put your ten pounds in the bank and let it make money. And he'll have a very good story to tell his friends."

"Oh dear!" said Hughie. "I think I'll go to bed. And you mustn't tell anyone about this, Alan."

"Rubbish! It shows that you're very kind to others."

Hughie left the club feeling very unhappy.

The next morning, an old man with gold glasses and grey hair came to Hughie's house.

"Are you Mr Hughie Erskine?" he asked.

"Yes," said Hughie.

"I have come from Baron Hausberg," said the grey-haired man. "The Baron asked me to bring you this letter."

On the outside of the letter was written, *For Hughie Erskine and Laura Merton on their marriage, from a poor old man,* and inside was a cheque for £10,000. Hughie and Laura were married soon after, and Alan Trevor and the "poor old man" were the happiest men in the church.

The Good Friend

Is anything more important than love? Some people say it is more important to be a good friend. But is it true? And what exactly is a good friend? Have you ever thought about it? Let me tell you a story that might help.

There was once a little man called Hans. He had a kind heart, and a round, happy face. He lived in a small house all alone. Every day he worked in his garden. It was the loveliest garden for far around. Every plant flowered at the right time. All the flowers looked beautiful, and smelled lovely.

Little Hans had a lot of friends. But his *best* friend was Hugh the Farmer. Every time Hugh passed Hans' garden he picked some flowers, or filled his pockets with fruit from the trees.

"Real friends should give each other everything they need," said Hugh.

Hugh grew a lot of food on his farm. He had six cows that give milk, and a lot of chickens. He was very rich. But he never gave

Hans anything from his farm. Neighbours sometimes thought this was strange, but Hans never worried about it. He loved listening to Hugh. Hugh often talked about the unselfishness of friends.

Little Hans worked in his garden. He was very happy during the spring, the summer and the autumn. But when the winter came, he had no fruit or flowers to take to market. He was often cold and hungry. Sometimes he went to bed without any food. In the winter he was very lonely because Hugh never came to see him.

Hugh said to his wife, "It's not necessary for me to go and see little Hans while the snow lasts. When people are in trouble, they should be left alone. Hans won't like me if I visit him now. That's how I think a friend should be, and I'm sure I'm right. I'll stay away from his house until spring. In the spring, he'll be able to give me plenty of flowers, then he'll be happy."

"You're certainly very thoughtful about other people," answered his wife, as she sat in her comfortable chair by the fire.

"But could we not ask little Hans to come up here?" said the Farmer's son. "If poor Hans is in trouble, I can give him half my soup."

"You *are* a strange boy!" cried the Farmer. "I don't see why we send you to school. You don't seem to learn anything. If Hans came to this house, he would see our food and our drink, and he would want it. That wouldn't be good for Hans. It would change his nature, and I couldn't let that happen. I am Hans's best friend."

"You speak very well," said the Farmer's wife.

"A lot of people act well, but few people talk well. Talking is much more difficult than *doing*," said the Farmer.

When the winter ended spring came, and the Farmer went to see Hans.

"You have a good heart," said the wife as he left. "Remember to take something to put the flowers in."

The Farmer went down the hill carrying a big box.

"Good morning, little Hans," said the Farmer.

"Good morning," said little Hans, smiling from ear to ear.

"And how have you been all winter?" asked the Farmer.

"Well, really," said Hans, "it's very good of you to ask. I had a very hard winter, but now the spring has come and I'm quite happy. All my flowers are doing well."

"We often talked about you during the winter, Hans," said the Farmer.

"That was kind of you," said Hans. "I thought you were forgetting me."

"Hans, I'm surprised at you," said the Farmer. "A friend never forgets. That is the wonderful thing about friends. They never forget. Your flowers are looking lovely."

"They certainly are lovely," said Hans. "And it's very lucky for me that I have so many. I am going to sell them at the market. Then I can buy back my wheelbarrow."

"Buy back your wheelbarrow? You didn't sell it, did you? How can you wheel heavy things about if you don't have a wheelbarrow?"

"Well, I had to sell it. The winter was very bad. I had no money to buy bread. First I sold my Sunday coat, then I sold my big pipe, and at last I sold my wheelbarrow. But I'm going to buy them all back again now."

"Hans," said the Farmer, "I will give you my wheelbarrow. It's not new; one side is gone, and there's something wrong with the wheel. But I'll give it to you. I know it's very kind of me. A lot of people will think I'm strange, but I'm not like the rest of the world. I'm happy to give it to you. I have a new wheelbarrow for myself, so it's easy."

"Well, that's very kind of you," said little Hans, and his face lit up with happiness. "I can easily fix the broken parts. I have some wood in the house."

"Some wood!" said the Farmer. "That's just what I need for my farm building. There's a large hole in the roof and I must fix it. It's lucky you mentioned it! I'm giving you my wheelbarrow and now you're going to give me your wood. Of course, the wheelbarrow is more valuable than the wood, but true friends don't notice things like that. Get the wood at once. Then I can start fixing the roof today."

"Certainly," cried Hans, and he ran and pulled out the wood.

"It's not a very big piece of wood," said the Farmer, looking at it. "When the roof is fixed there won't be enough for the wheelbarrow. But of course, I can't help that. Now, I've given you my wheelbarrow. I'm sure you'd like to give me some flowers in return. Here's the box. Please be sure to fill it to the top!"

"To the top?" said little Hans, sadly.

It was a very big box. If he filled it to the top, he would have no flowers left for the market. He really wanted to buy back his pipe and his Sunday coat.

"Well, really," said the Farmer. "I've given you my wheelbarrow. All I want are a few flowers. I thought true friends were free from selfishness of any kind."

"My dear friend, my best friend," cried little Hans, "you're welcome to take all the flowers in my garden. I like hearing your good

57

thoughts. They're better than my coat and my pipe."

Then Hans ran and picked flowers and filled the Farmer's box.

"Goodbye, little Hans," said the Farmer as he went up the hill with the wood on his back and the box full of flowers.

"Goodbye," said little Hans, and he began to happily dig his garden again. He was thinking about the wheelbarrow.

The next day, he was tying up some big flowers against the wall of the house. He heard the Farmer's voice from the road. Hans looked over the wall. The Farmer was standing there with a large bag on his back.

"Dear little Hans," said the Farmer, "could you carry this bag to the market for me?"

"Oh, I'm sorry," said little Hans, "but I'm very busy today. I have to tie up these plants against the wall, and water the flowers and cut all my grass."

"Well, really," said the Farmer, "I think it's very unfriendly to refuse. After all, I'm going to give you my wheelbarrow."

"Oh, don't say that," cried little Hans, "I don't want to be unfriendly." He quickly put on his hat, and went off to market with the big bag on his back.

It was a very hot day and the road was very dusty. Hans walked with difficulty, but at last he reached the market. After some time he sold the Farmer's big bag and everything in it. He got a good price. Then he returned home as quickly as he could. He was afraid that thieves on the road might steal the Farmer's money.

"It's been a hard day," said Hans to himself, as he was going to bed that night. "But I didn't refuse the Farmer. And that's good. He's my best friend. And he's going to give me his wheelbarrow."

Early next morning the Farmer came to get the money for his bag of things. But little Hans was very tired – he was still in bed.

"I'm very sorry," said little Hans sleepily. "But I'm really tired. I wanted to lie in bed for some time. I always work better after I've heard the birds singing."

"Well, I am pleased about that," said the Farmer. "I want you to come to my farm this morning. You can fix the roof for me."

Poor little Hans really wanted to work in his garden. His flowers needed water. But he didn't like to refuse the Farmer. The Farmer was such a good friend to him.

"Can I come another day, when I'm not so busy?" asked little Hans in a small voice.

"Well, really," answered the Farmer, "it's not much to ask of you. Remember – I'm going to give you my wheelbarrow. But, of course, if you refuse, I'll go and do it myself."

"Oh no!" cried little Hans. He jumped out of bed and dressed and went to the farm.

He worked all day. At sunset, the Farmer came to see his work.

"Have you fixed the hole in the roof?" cried the Farmer.

"Yes, it's completely fixed now," answered little Hans, coming down from the roof.

"Ah!" said the Farmer, "the work that a man does for others – that's the best work."

"It's very nice hearing you talking," answered little Hans. "But I'll never have such nice ideas as you have."

"Oh! They'll come to you," said the Farmer, "but you must take more care. It's easy to be a friend if you know the rules."

"Do you really think I can learn the rules?" asked little Hans.

"Oh, yes," said the Farmer. "But you've fixed my roof and now you must go home and rest. I want you to take my cows to the mountain tomorrow."

Poor little Hans was afraid to say no. The Farmer brought his cows to Hans' house early next morning. Hans started off for the mountain at once. It took him the whole day to get there and back. When he returned, he was very tired. He went to sleep in his chair, and he didn't wake up until the next morning.

"I'll have a nice time in my garden today," he said to himself, when he woke up.

But he was never able to look after his flowers. His friend the Farmer was always coming to his house. He always wanted Hans to do something. The Farmer always had a job for Hans.

Little Hans was very worried – his flowers needed care. His garden couldn't grow without him.

But then he said to himself, "The Farmer is going to give me his wheelbarrow. That is very, very kind of him."

So Hans worked and worked for the Farmer. The Farmer said a lot of things about friends. Friends were very important, he said.

One night Hans was sitting by his fire at home. He heard a loud noise at the door. It was a wild night, and the wind was blowing around the house. At first, Hans thought it was only the storm. But the noise continued.

"It's a poor traveller," said little Hans to himself, and he ran to the door.

The Farmer was standing there, with a light in one hand and a big stick in the other.

"Dear little Hans," cried the Farmer, "I'm in great trouble. My little boy has fallen and hurt himself. I'm going for the Doctor. But he lives very far away, and it's a bad night. Will *you* go and get him? You know I'm going to give you my wheelbarrow. It's only fair that you do something for me in return."

"Certainly," cried little Hans. "I'm very glad you asked me. I'll go at once. But you must give me your light. It's a dark night and I'm afraid I might fall."

"I'm very sorry," answered the Farmer, "but it's my new light. I don't want anything to happen to it."

"Well, it doesn't matter then. I'll manage without it," cried little Hans. He took his big coat and his warm red hat, and left the house.

It was a wild storm! It was very dark, and the sky was black. Hans couldn't see very much. The wind was strong and it was difficult to stand up. But he arrived at the Doctor's house after three hours.

"What do you want, little Hans?" asked the Doctor.

"The Farmer's son has fallen and hurt himself. The Farmer wants you to come at once."

"All right," said the Doctor. He got out his horse and his winter shoes and his light. And then he rode off in the direction of the Farmer's house.

Little Hans walked behind him, with great difficulty.

The storm grew worse and worse. The cold rain fell heavily, and Hans could not see the road. At last he lost his way. He slowly walked far from the road, and he came to a dangerous place. The ground was very wet – and there was a lot of water in deep holes. Poor little Hans fell into the water.

The next day, some boys found his body. He was dead after a night in the cold weather. The boys took him to his little house.

Everybody went to the church three days later. Everybody liked Hans, and it was a sad day for the villagers.

The Farmer said, "I was his best friend, so I must have the best place."

So he walked at the head of the crowd in a long black coat. From time to time, he put his hand to his eyes.

After the church, everybody talked about Hans.

"Little Hans is certainly a great loss to everybody," said one villager.

"A great loss to me, certainly." answered the Farmer; "I nearly gave him my wheelbarrow, and now I don't know what to do with it. I have nowhere to keep it. It's broken, so I can't sell it. I'll certainly take care not to give away anything again. If you are kind to people you always have troubles."

Well? Is a good friend the most important thing in the world? Would the Farmer agree? Would Little Hans agree? Would *you* agree?

WORDGAME

Answer these clues and find what the sad student wanted. Write the answers in the boxes.

1 The Nightingale pressed against this.
2 The Nightingale sang of _____.
3 The Happy Prince gave this to the poor people of the town.
4 Who came to play in the Giant's garden?
5 The fortune-teller's name?
6 The "poor old man" was wearing very old _____.
7 Little Hans loved to work here.

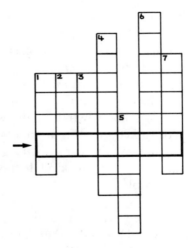